The Epistle to the Laodiceans

A Rediscovered Letter of Paul
- A Modern Translation -
Adapted for the Contemporary
Reader

A Modern Translation
Adapted for the Contemporary
Reader

Anonymous
(Apocryphal Pauline Letter,
4th Century CE)

Translated by Tim Zengerink

© **Copyright 2025**
All rights reserved.

It is not legal to reproduce, duplicate, or transmit any part of this document in either electronic means or in printed format. Recording of this publication is strictly prohibited and any storage of this document is not allowed unless with written permission from the publisher except for the use of brief quotations in a book review.

This book contains works of fiction. Any resemblance to persons living or dead, or places, events, or locations is purely coincidental.

Table of Contents

Preface - Message to the Reader..................1

Introduction 6

The Epistle of Paul The Apostle to
    The Laodiceans...................................... 11

Thank You for Reading............................. 14

Preface - Message to the Reader

What If You Could Help Rebuild the Greatest Library in Human History?

Thousands of years ago, the Library of Alexandria stood as the crown jewel of human achievement — a sanctuary where the collected wisdom of every known civilization was gathered, preserved, and shared freely.

And then, it was lost.

Through fire, conquest, and the slow erosion of time, humanity lost not just books — but ideas, dreams, discoveries, and stories that could have changed the world forever.

Today, the Library of Alexandria lives again — and you are invited to be a part of its restoration.

Our mission is simple yet profound:

To rebuild the greatest library the world has ever known, and to translate all timeless works into every language and dialect, so that no seeker of knowledge is ever left behind again.

By joining our movement to rebuild the modern Library of Alexandria, you become part of an unprecedented mission:

- **Unlimited Access to the Greatest Audiobooks & eBooks Ever Written:**

    Instantly explore thousands of legendary works—Plato, Shakespeare, Jane Austen, Leo Tolstoy, and countless more. All instantly available to read or listen, placing a complete literary universe at your fingertips.

- **Beautiful Paperback & Deluxe Editions at Printing Cost**

    Own any title as an elegant paperback, deluxe hardcover, or stunning collectible boxset—offered to you at true printing cost, delivered straight to your door. Build your personal Library of Alexandria, crafted for beauty, built for durability, and worthy of proud display.

- **Fresh Translations for Modern Readers—in Every Language & Dialect**

    Enjoy timeless masterpieces reimagined in clear, contemporary language—no more outdated phrases or obscure references. Alongside the original versions, we're tirelessly translating these classics into every language and dialect imaginable, ensuring accessibility and understanding across cultures and generations.

- **Join a Global Renaissance of Literature & Knowledge**

    You directly support expanding our library, publishing deluxe editions at true cost, translating works into all global languages, and bringing humanity's greatest stories to people everywhere. By joining today, you're not just preserving a legacy of masterpieces; you set in motion a powerful wave of literary accessibility.

Become a Torchbearer of Knowledge.

Join us for free now at **LibraryofAlexandria.com**

Together, we will ensure that the light of human wisdom never fades again.

With gratitude and a shared love of knowledge,
The Modern Library of Alexandria Team

Visit:

www.libraryofalexandria.com

Or scan the code below:

Introduction

Reclaiming a Forgotten Voice: Faith, Grace, and Unity in the Spirit of Paul

Among the many texts that orbit the canon of early Christian writings, The Epistle to the Laodiceans holds a peculiar place—one marked by intrigue, controversy, and enduring fascination. Although not found in the official New Testament, this short epistle has appeared in various manuscripts and translations throughout history, often nestled among the letters of Paul. It has been included in many editions of the Latin Vulgate, cited in medieval Christian literature, and even preserved in the historical memory of the Church. Though modern scholars widely regard it as apocryphal—likely written in the 4th century CE and not by Paul himself—it nonetheless captures something deeply resonant with the apostle's voice: a call to unity, perseverance, and unwavering faith.

The origin of this letter is shrouded in mystery. It was possibly written to fill a perceived gap in the biblical record. In his letter to the Colossians (Colossians 4:16), Paul refers to a letter to the Laodiceans that they were to read, alongside the one sent to them. This passing reference, though brief, ignited centuries of speculation: What happened to that letter? Was it lost? Was it suppressed? Or could it be the very epistle preserved under this name?

While we may never know the full story, what we do have is a brief but stirring piece of spiritual writing that reflects Pauline style and themes. The letter emphasizes core Christian teachings: the grace of God, the power of the resurrection, the call to unity, and the need to remain steadfast in love and righteousness. It lacks some of the theological complexity and specific instructions found in Paul's authentic epistles, but it compensates with clarity of purpose and spiritual encouragement.

In a world increasingly fragmented—by politics, ideology, and spiritual confusion—The Epistle to the Laodiceans speaks with striking relevance. It calls believers to hold fast to the message of Christ, to embody the fruits of the Spirit, and to remember the grace that first called them to faith. It reminds readers that the foundation of Christian life is not human wisdom or worldly power, but the simple, transformative truth of the gospel. Whether penned by Paul or by a later admirer in his name, this epistle remains a spiritual gem—brief, radiant, and full of light.

A Letter for the Modern Church

For contemporary readers, The Epistle to the Laodiceans offers a rare opportunity to reengage with the Pauline tradition in a fresh and meaningful way. Its message is not bound by ancient polemics or ecclesial disputes, but instead focused on the essentials: grace, faith, perseverance, and the unity of believers in Christ. It speaks directly to the heart of the Church's mission in every age: to live out the gospel with joy, humility, and integrity.

The letter opens with praise for the grace that comes through Jesus Christ and immediately grounds the reader in the reality of the resurrection. This is a faith not rooted in sentiment or tradition alone, but in the living truth of the risen Christ. The writer reminds the Laodiceans—and by extension, us—that spiritual strength comes not from ritual observance but from a living relationship with God.

Throughout the letter, echoes of Pauline phrases and rhythms are unmistakable. Phrases such as "stand fast in the Lord," "let all things be done in love," and "rejoice always in Christ" remind us of the ethical and spiritual exhortations found in authentic Pauline letters like Philippians, Thessalonians, and Galatians. The emphasis is not on intellectual abstraction or institutional structures, but on the lived reality of the Spirit among the faithful.

This modern adaptation has been crafted to bring the clarity, rhythm, and intent of the original text into contemporary language. Where archaic expressions obscured meaning, clarity has been restored. Where phrasing was rigid or unfamiliar, it has been softened to make

Translated by Tim Zengerink

space for deeper reflection. Yet, the message remains the same: to call the Church to its true center, to lift the eyes of the believer back to the source of all hope.

Whether you read this epistle as a historical curiosity, a spiritual meditation, or an authentic word of encouragement, you are invited into a conversation that spans centuries. The Epistle to the Laodiceans reminds us that what endures in faith is not form but essence—not the letter, but the Spirit. It asks us to return to the heart of the gospel: grace given, love shared, and joy made full in Christ.

May this book renew your faith, sharpen your vision, and strengthen your walk with God. In a time where many voices clamor for attention, may the quiet authority of this lost epistle once again lead us toward the unity, peace, and steadfast hope that are the hallmarks of true Christian life.

The Epistle of Paul The Apostle to The Laodiceans

From Paul, an apostle—not chosen by people or appointed by any man, but called by Jesus Christ—to the believers in Laodicea:

I pray that God our Father and the Lord Jesus Christ will give you grace and peace.

Every time I pray, I thank Jesus Christ for you. I ask that you keep doing good and stay strong in your faith, as you wait for what God has promised to give on the day of judgment.

Don't let anyone's empty words confuse you or pull you away from the truth of the Good News I shared with you.

I ask God to help all who believe through my message to fully understand the truth of the Gospel, to be kind, and to keep doing good things that show they are saved.

Translated by Tim Zengerink

I'm in prison because of Christ, and everyone knows it. But I'm happy and thankful even in these chains.

I believe this will lead to my eternal salvation, helped by your prayers and the Holy Spirit.

Whether I live or die, I live for Christ—and if I die, that will be even better.

I trust that our Lord will be kind and help you love each other and be united in how you think and live.

So, dear friends, since you've heard that the Lord is coming, live with respect and reverence. This will lead to eternal life.

Remember—it is God who is working in you.

So do everything without sin.

Most importantly, my dear friends, be joyful in Jesus Christ, and stay away from greedy or dishonest gain.

Tell God everything you need. Stay true to the teachings of Christ.

Focus your mind on what is true, good, pure, just, and beautiful. Do these things.

Keep thinking about the teachings you've heard and accepted, and you will have peace.

All the believers send their greetings.

May the grace of our Lord Jesus Christ be with your spirit. Amen.

Make sure this letter is read to the church in Colossae, and read their letter in your church too.

Thank You for Reading

Dear Reader,

We hope this timeless classic has sparked your imagination and enriched your literary journey. Now that you've turned the final page, we want to share a vision for the future of reading—one where every classic you've ever wanted to explore is at your fingertips, in a format that best suits your life.

We'd like to invite you to gain immediate, unlimited digital & audiobook access to hundreds of the most treasured literary classics ever written—along with the option to secure deluxe paperback, hardcover & box set editions at printing cost. Together, we can spark a new global literary renaissance alongside our small, independent publishing house called "The Library of Alexandria."

Thousands of years ago, the Library of Alexandria stood as a beacon of knowledge—until it was lost to history. We aim to reignite that spirit of preservation and discovery right now, in the modern age—only this time, it's accessible to all, in every language and every format.

Picture a world where every timeless classic, novel, poem, or philosophical treatise is not only available to read but also updated for today's readers—modernized, translated into any language or dialect, and ready to enjoy in any format you choose, whether that is in an eBook, audiobook, paperback, or deluxe hardcover & box set version a printing cost.

By joining our movement to rebuild the modern Library of Alexandria, you become part of an unprecedented mission to offer:

- **Unlimited Audiobook & eBook Access to the Greatest Classics of All Time**

    Instantly explore thousands of legendary works, from Plato and Shakespeare to Jane Austen and Leo Tolstoy. All are instantly ready to read or listen to, giving you a complete literary universe at your fingertips.

- **Paperback & Deluxe Editions at Printing Costs:**

  Purchase any title in a paperback, deluxe hardbound, or deluxe boxset edition at printing costs, shipped right to your doorstep. Curate your personal library of Alexandria with editions worthy of display—crafted to last, designed to captivate, and delivered straight to your door.

- **Modern translations for Contemporary Readers in all languages and dialects**

  Discover a vast selection of classics reimagined in clear, current language—no more struggling with outdated phrases or obscure references. Next to the original versions, we aim to offer translations in as many languages and dialects as possible.

  As we continue our translation efforts and add new languages, readers everywhere can connect with these works as if they were written today. By bridging linguistic divides, you're contributing to ensuring that these timeless stories become more meaningful, accessible, and inspiring for people across the globe.

- **Your Personal Library of Alexandria:**

    Over the months and years, you'll curate a unique physical archive of classics—each volume a testament to your taste, curiosity, and love of knowledge. It's not just about owning books—it's about curating a cultural legacy you'll cherish and pass down for generations to come.

- **Join a Global Literary Renaissance:**

    Your support fuels an ongoing mission: allowing us to reinvest in offering deluxe print editions (including special boxsets) at their true cost, broaden the range of available formats and translations, and extend the reach of these works to new audiences worldwide. By joining today, you're not just preserving a legacy of masterpieces;

you set in motion a powerful wave of literary accessibility.

We are more than a publisher—we're a movement, and we can't do it alone. Your support lets us scale our mission, preserving and reimagining history's greatest works for tomorrow's readers.

Become a Torchbearer of knowledge.

Thank you for picking up this book and allowing us into your literary journey. As you turn the pages, know that you're part of something larger: a global effort to keep these stories alive, share their wisdom across borders and generations, and spark a true cultural revival for the modern era.

If this resonates with you—please consider taking the next step by visiting:

www.libraryofalexandria.com

With gratitude and a shared love of knowledge,

The Modern Library of Alexandria Team

Visit:

www.libraryofalexandria.com

Or scan the code below:

www.ingramcontent.com/pod-product-compliance
Lightning Source LLC
LaVergne TN
LVHW030632080426
835512LV00021B/3473